NEGRO AUTHORS AND COMPOSERS
OF THE UNITED STATES

AMS PRESS
NEW YORK

NEGRO AUTHORS AND COMPOSERS

OF THE UNITED STATES

By W. C. Handy

Publishers

HANDY BROTHERS MUSIC CO. INC.

1587 Broadway, New York, N. Y.

Library of Congress Cataloging in Publication Data

Handy, William Christopher, 1873-1958.
Negro authors and composers of the United States.

Reprint of the 1938? ed. published by Handy Bros.
Music Co., New York.
1. Afro-American musicians—Biography. 2. Afro-
American authors—Biography. I. Title.
ML3556.H23N3   1976   780'.92'2 [B]   74-24105
ISBN 0-404-12953-6

Reprinted from an original copy in the collections
of the Ohio State University Library

From the edition of 1938, New York
First AMS edition published in 1976
Manufactured in the United States of America

AMS PRESS INC.
NEW YORK, N. Y.

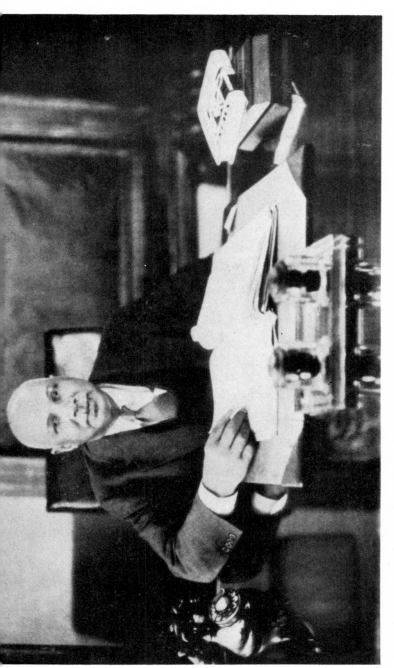

NEGRO AUTHORS AND COMPOSERS OF THE UNITED STATES

By W. C. HANDY

NEGRO AUTHORS AND COMPOSERS
OF THE UNITED STATES

(a—author; c—composer; *—deceased; ASCAP—Member of the American Society of Composers, Authors and Publishers)

The Negro Composer has contributed in a large measure to the long list of popular and classic American music, some of whose names are almost forgotten.

Do you know that Gussie L. Davis*(c) who wrote more than 600 popular songs such as "The Light House By The Sea," "The Fatal Wedding," "The Baggage Coach Ahead," "My Creole Sue," was a Negro?

That James Bland*(c) was one of our group and his song, "Carry Me Back To Ole Virginny," will probably live as long as there is a Virginia.

Do you know that "Listen To The Mocking Bird" like many other songs was composed by a Negro who did not write the music? The Composer of "Listen To The Mocking Bird" was a Philadelphia Negro, whose song found its way into the Guitar Method of Septimus Winner. How strange it is that a beautiful song written by a Negro that grips the heart of American music lovers loses its racial identity without the least regard.

A few of the numbers listed as compositions of Race Composers had as collaborators white Authors and Composers whose names we omit.

Handy Brothers Music Co. Inc., is putting forth strenuous efforts to build a catalog from the pen of talented Negro Composers. 1935 saw a splendid fulfillment of a dream of W. C. Handy, founder of this well known Institution. For in this year more compositions in this category were published than any other year in his quarter century of publishing.

The success of this endeavor depends upon your appreciation of this movement, your encouragement and patronage. Hence, the purpose of this list, to keep alive the memory of those who have left us such a worthy heritage and to acquaint you with contemporary writers who may leave their "foot prints on the sands of time."

Many of the worlds greatest composers have written beautiful songs that have made the world a better place in which to live, yet for themselves received very little encouragement and small remuneration. Some barely missed the pauper's grave.

In New York City, 1914, an organization was formed to bring Authors and Composers of Music into a closer relationship without regard to race, creed or color and to protect their rights against prevailing social abuses. This organization is now known as "The American Society of Composers, Authors and Publishers," with a membership of more than 1,000 and collects a fee for performance/ of copyrighted music for profit from radio stations, dance halls, picture houses and other amusement places. The funds derived therefrom are distributed quarterly among the Composers, Authors and Publishers.

We present a few of the names of members of our group who are or were members of this organization but whose compositions we do not publish:

BURLEIGH, HARRY T.(c), better known for his spiritual arrangement of "Deep River," "Jean," "Ethiopia Saluting The Colors," "Just You," etc.

COOK, WILL MARION(c), "Clorenda," "Exhortation," "Emancipation Day" and much of the music for the "Williams and Walker" shows, also his own productions.

DETT, R. NATHANIEL(c), better known for his excellent choral arrangements, most popular of which is "Listen To The Lamb"; "Juba Dance" from the Suite—In the Bottoms.

ELLINGTON, DUKE(c), "Mood Indigo," "Sophisticated Lady," "Black and Tan Fantasy."

J. C. JOHNSON(c), "Traveling," "Don't Let Your Love Go Wrong," "Believe It, Beloved," "Rhythm and Romance," "Deep Dawn."

JOHNSON, JAMES WELDON(c), Poet, one of America's foremost writers who in collaboration with his brother, J. ROSAMOND JOHNSON, a member of the song writing team of "Cole and Johnson," wrote many international "hits" in the late 90's and will be remembered best by the Negro National Anthem, "Lift Every Voice and Sing."

MCPHERSON, CECIL (Cecil Mack)(a). Founder of the Gotham Attucks Music Publishing Co., the first publishing company to be owned and operated by Negroes in New York. Author of "Down Among The Sugar Cane," "Teasing," "You're In The Right Church But The Wrong Pew," "He's A Cousin of Mine."

SWEATMAN, WILBUR C.(c), "Down Home Rag," "Battle-ship Kate," "Virginia Diggins," "Old Folks Rag," "That's Got 'Em," etc.
TRENT, JOE(a), "Muddy Water," "Feelin' High."

3

TYERS, WILLIAM H.*(c), a South American who became naturalized and wrote such beautiful numbers as "Maori," "Panama," "Admiration, "Call of The Woods Waltz," "La Trocha." He was the foremost writer of Tango Music in America.

WALLER, THOMAS (FATS)(c), "I Got A Feelin' I'm Fallin'," "Honey Suckle Rose," "Ain't Misbehavin'," "My Fate Is In Your Hands."

WILLIAMS, CLARENCE is one of our foremost music publishers and composer of "Brownskin," "Royal Garden Blues," "Ain't Gonna Give Nobody None O' This Jelly Roll," "Shout Sister Shout," "Sugar Blues," etc.

LIST OF COMPOSITIONS BY RACE COMPOSERS

Published by

HANDY BROTHERS MUSIC CO. INC.

Classification

OPERATIC COMPOSERS

"WHITHER?"—G Sharp
"IF THOU DIDST LOVE"—G Flat

H. Lawrence Freeman(c), born in Cleveland, Ohio. 1902-4, Head of Music Department, Wilberforce University. Has written and produced 14 operas and received the Harmon Award for his operas "Voodoo" and "The Octoroon" in 1930.

"I PROMISE"—A Flat
(For Wedding Ceremonies)

Shirley Graham McCanns(c) has the distinction of being the first colored woman in America to successfully produce an opera, the title of which was "Tom Tom," Cleveland, Ohio.

COMPOSERS OF CONCERT MUSIC

"LI'L' BLACK CHILD"
"THE CITY OF JASPER WALLS"

Wellington Adams (c), First Rodman Wanamaker Prize Winner; U. S., Geo. Washington Bicentennial Composer; Music Editor, Baptist Standard Hymnal; Formerly Editor and Publisher of The Music Master Magazine; Charter Member of The National Association of Negro Musicians, Inc. His other compositions include: "Hymn To Freedom," "Shine, Oh, Shine," and "The Newborn King." He is listed among the nine (9) leading Afro-American Composers in "Modern

Music and Musicians Encyclopedia, Vol. I, Philharmonic Edition on Great Composers.

"TRADITION"
(Can Be Staged with esthetic dancers).

Ismay Andrews(c), a talented actress and musician whose song has been dramatized with tremendous success in the concert halls of New York.

"LAZ'RUS"—From "Blow Gabriel Blow"
(A descriptive Biblical story—8 pages, for robusto tenor or baritone.)

Donald Heywood(ASCAP), a graduate of Fisk University who has written and produced in New York several musical comedies, better known of which are: "Ole Man Satan," "Hot Rhythm," "Africana." He is the author of "I'm Comin' Virginia."

"A SONG" (How The First Song Was Born)
     C and F.

ALEXANDER HILL*(ASCAP), born in Little Rock, Ark. The son of a Methodist minister. He wrote more than a hundred songs.

"VESUVIUS" (There's a Red Glow In The Sky Above Vesuvius)
(An Universal Plea for Peace).
     Poem by Andy Razaf (ASCAP).
     Music by W. C. Handy (ASCAP).

"TOOK MAH BABE AWAY"—G
(A Negro Lamentation).

J. Milton Reddie, born in Baltimore, Md. A rising young poet.

ARRANGERS OF SPIRITUALS

Mixed Voices

"DOWN IN THE VALLEY AWAITING FOR MY JESUS"

W. Arthur Calhoun was Roland Hayes' first teacher.

"STEAL AWAY TO JESUS"
"LET US CHEER THE WEARY TRAVELER"
"GIVE ME JESUS"
"STAND ON THE ROCK A LITTLE LONGER"
"I'VE HEARD OF A CITY CALLED HEAVEN"

"I'M FEELIN' DEVILISH"
"SUGAR" (That Sugar Baby O'Mine)
"IT'S JUST A STATE OF MIND"

Maceo Pinkard(ASCAP) is the writer of "Mammy O'Mine," "Sweet Georgia Brown," "Congratulations." Other numbers published from his pen are:

"YOU'RE IN WRONG WITH THE RIGHT BABY"
"YOU CAN'T TELL THE DIFFERENCE AFTER DARK"
"ANYTIME"

"BOODLE-AM"
"GIVE ME JUST A LITTLE BIT OF YOUR LOVE"
"RINGTAIL BLUES"
"THE BLUES SINGER FROM ALABAM"
"WHO'S THAT MAN"
"I NEVER HAD THE BLUES UNTIL I LEFT OLD
    DIXIELAND"

Spencer Williams(ASCAP) is the writer of "Everybody Loves My Baby," "Tishmingo Blues," "I Ain't Got Nobody," "Royal Garden Blues." He is a native of New Orleans, now residing in Paris, France.

"JAZZBO JOHNSON'S SYNCOPATING BAND"
W. Benton Overstreet(c) is the writer of "There'll Be Some Changes Made" and "Jazz Dance," recorded on Columbia Records by Handy's band in 1917.

"IF YOU DON'T LIKE MY PEACHES DON'T SHAKE MY TREE,"
    Alonzo Govern(c).
"WOULDN'T THAT BE A DREAM," "TAKE YOUR TIME,"
"SWEETIE DEAR," "LOVIE JOE," Joe Jordan(c).

Mr. Jordan is a successful orchestra leader and showman both in America and abroad.

"REMEMBER AND BE CAREFUL EVERY DAY"
    Tom Lemonier is the author of "Just One Word Of Consolation."
    Lew Payton(c) is a well known actor on stage and screen.

"I LIKE YOU BECAUSE YOU HAVE SUCH LOVING
    WAYS"

6

Noah Francis Ryder, a Hampton product and choral director.

"I WANT JESUS TO WALK WITH ME"
"SIT DOWN"
"HOLD THE WIND"
"MY WAY IS CLOUDY"
"FOUR AND TWENTY ELDERS"
"GOING TO HOLD OUT TO THE END"
"SIN-TRYING WORLD"
"PALE HORSE AND RIDER"

Jean Stor, a successful choral director.

"DEEP RIVER"
Wen Talbert, a well known bandmaster and choral director.

Male Quartet

"TIME AIN'T LONG"
"DERE'S A MAN GOIN' 'ROUND TAKIN' NAMES"
"REMEMBER AND BE CAREFUL EVERY DAY"

William C. Elkins, a well known director of Glee clubs in Washington and New York.

"WHEN THE BLACK MAN HAS A NATION OF HIS OWN"
(Solo—male quartet)

By J. M. Miller and W. C. Handy.

MUSICAL COMEDY COMPOSERS

"BLUE THOUGHTS" (Piano Solo)
"TRUCKIN' ON DOWN"
"IT AIN'T BEING DONE NO MORE"
"CARELESS LOVE" (Piano Transcription)

Eubie Blake (ASCAP) of "Sissle and Blake" fame produced the musical comedy success "Shuffle Along." He composed many songs, better known of which are: "Love Will Find A Way," "I'm Just Wild About Harry," "Bandana Days," "Memories Of You."

"POLKA DOT STOMP"
"UNDER THE DREAMY CREOLE MOON"

Noble Sissle (ASCAP), Sidney Bechet, James Tolliver. These numbers have frequently been heard on records and over the radio.

"OH, SING A NEW SONG"

Noble Sissle(ASCAP) and Will Vodery.

Mr. Sissle successfully staged the Negro Pageant, "Oh Sing A New Song" in Chicago, 1934. He was with the late James Reese Europe over seas in the World's War.

Mr. Vodery (c) wrote many beautiful orchestrations and much of the music for Ziegfeld's Follies. His other compositions include: "Tomorrow," "When I Return," "Dearest Memories," "Come Down And Kiss Me Stella," etc.

"Harlem Hotcha"

"AINTCHA GOT MUSIC"
"THERE GOES MY HEADACHE"
"I WAS SO WEAK LOVE WAS SO STRONG"
"YOURS ALL YOURS"
"STOP THAT DOG"

James P. Johnson(ASCAP) famous as a Q.R.S. recording artist on Player Piano Rolls, wrote "Old Fashion Love" and "If I Could Be With You," which are popular songs even today. "Carolina Shout" and later piano solos were also current record hits. He composed the world famous "Charleston" and was the first one to start musical synchronization for colored shorts with "Miller and Lyles." His "Yama Kraw" is a genuine Negro Rhapsody In Blue.

Andy Razaf(ASCAP) who wrote the lyrics of the "Harlem Hotcha" tunes is the author of "Supposin'," "Ain't Misbehavin'," "My Fate Is In Your Hands," "Dusky Stevedor," "Handy Man." He is a poet whose writings have enjoyed wide popularity. Other lyrics from his pen published by us are:

"STAY"
"MY JOE LOUIS OF LOVE"

"I'M LOOKING ALL AROUND FOR A VAMPIRE"

Henry Creamer*(ASCAP) wrote "Sweet Emilina My Gal," "Way Down Yonder In New Orleans," "After You've Gone," etc. Mr. Creamer and Mr. Layton were responsible for the score of Mr. and Mrs. Coburn's "Three Showers," once popular on Broadway.

Mr. Layton(c) is well known in London thru the team of "Johnston and Layton."

COMPOSERS OF POPULAR MUSIC

"IT'S THE VOICE OF OLD MAN RIVER"

Harry White(c) and Willie Bryant. Victor record No. 25129B.

"WONDERIN' WHY I'M LONESOME"

Lem Fowler(c), "He May Be Your Man But He Comes To See Me Sometime."

"SLIDING FEVERS"
"SOUTHERN MEMORIES" (band)

Alex M. Valentine(c) was formerly a teacher of music at Bordentown Manual Training School, Bordentown, N. J.

"THERE MUST BE SOMETHING WRONG WITH ME"

Freddie Johnson(c) and Harry A. DeMund(c), vaudeville artists.

"YOU'RE JUST A LITTLE FLOWER THAT THE
    BEES HAVEN'T FOUND"
"EVERYTHING HAPPENS JUST PLEASES ME"

Russell Smith(c), vaudeville artist.

"ALIBI-ING PAPA"
"SWEET MAMA GOODIE"

Tyus and Tyus(c), recording and stage artists.

"AIN'T MUCH GOOD IN THE BEST OF MEN NOW DAYS"

Eugene Hunter(c).

"BROADWAY RHYTHM"
"HE BURNS ME UP, AND HE KNOCKS ME COLD!"

Millard G. Thomas(c).

"I'M GOING BACK TO MY USED TO BE"
"I'M GOING OUT TONIGHT TO STRUT MY STUFF"

Jimmy Cox (c).

"NO NAME WALTZ"
"ELYSIAN WALTZ"
"PREPAREDNESS BLUES"
"THOUGH WE'RE MILES AND MILES APART"

Charles Warren Hillman*(c) was the first pianist with Handy's band of Memphis.

"ALLIES TRIUMPHAL MARCH"
"MAUVOLEYNE WALTZ"

Frederick Bryan*(c) was pianist and former conductor of the Clef Club and wrote in collaboration with Alex Rogers, "Dancin' Deacon."

Mr. Rogers*(c) was responsible for many of Broadway's Musical Comedy successes. He wrote most of the material for the immortal Bert Williams.

"SWING THAT THING"
"AFTER ALL THESE YEARS"

Shelton Brooks(ASCAP) is the writer of "Some Of These Days," "Darktown Strutter's Ball," "Walkin' The Dog," "All Night Long," etc. He is a successful showman.

"HARLEM" (HARLEM'S HEAVEN TO ME)

Arthur Porter(a) and Edgar Dowell(c).

Mr. Dowell has written many revues.
Mr. Porter appeared in the stage and screen versions of "The "Green Pastures." He is the author of:

"TRUCKIN' ON DOWN"
"MOZAMBIQUE"

"THE SPHINX"
"WHY DID YOU MAKE A PLAYTHING OF ME"

J. Berni Barbour(c).

"TOOT TOOT DIXIE BOUND IN THE MORNING"

Lieut. J. Tim Brymn(ASCAP) and Chris Smith(ASCAP). J. Tim Brymn is the composer of "Please Go Away and Let Me Sleep," "Josephine My Joe," and the author of "Aunt Hager's Children" in collaboration with W. C. Handy. He was leader of the 350th Field Artillery Band during the World's War.

Chris Smith(ASCAP) is one of the most prolific writers in America. He wrote "Ballin' The Jack," "You're In The Right Church But The Wrong Pew," "He's A Cousin Of Mine," "Down Among The Sugar Cane," "Long Gone" (From Bowlin' Green), "Good Morning Carrie," "After All That I've Been To You," "Birth of Jazz," "Who Was The Husband Of Aunt Jemima" (The Mammy Of The Gold Dust Twins), etc.

"OH YOU DARKTOWN REGIMENTAL BAND"

"I'M DRINKING FROM A FOUNTAIN THAT NEVER
    RUNS DRY"
"WE'LL GO ON AND SERVE THE LORD"
"I'LL BE THERE IN THE MORNING"
"HIST DE WINDOW NOAH"
"NO MORE, NO MORE, NO MORE MY LORD
    I'LL NEVER TURN BACK NO MORE"
"'TIS THE OLD SHIP OF ZION"
"THAT OTHER WORLD IS NOT LIKE THIS"
                or
"TELL ALL THE WORLD JOHN"
"THE BRIDEGROOM HAS DONE COME"
By W. C. Handy

———

"JOSHUA FIT DE BATTLE O' JERICO"
"NOW LET ME FLY"
"STEAL AWAY TO JESUS"
"SAME TRAIN"
"GO, CHAIN DE LION DOWN"
"O, WASN'T THAT A WIDE RIVER"
"O, COME LET US SING" (From Pageant, "O, Sing A New Song")

J. Rosamond Johnson (ASCAP) in collaboration with Robert Cole
wrote the following shows: "Red Moon," "Shoo Fly Regiment," "Bert
Williams' 'Mr. Load Of Koal'." His best known songs are "Under
The Bamboo Tree," "In My Castle On The River Nile," "The Maiden
With The Dreamy Eyes," "Li'l Gal," "The Awakening."

———

"HOLD ON"
"WADE IN DE WATER"

Kaye Parker has arranged many excellent choral arrangements
in the leading broadcasting organizations.

———

"O' LEM'ME SHINE"
"GWINE UP"
"GONNA JOURNEY AWAY"
"I WILL NEVER BETRAY MY LORD"
"RUN TO JESUS"
"I HEARD THE PREACHING OF THE ELDER"
"NOBODY KNOWS DE TROUBLE I SEE"
"IN BRIGHT MANSIONS ABOVE"
"BALM IN GILEAD"
"I GOT A MOTHER IN THE HEAVEN"
"GREAT DAY"

Farrell(c) and Hatch(c) are the authors of "Lucy," "Mamma And Papa Blues," etc. They were headline attractions in the days of vaudeville. Mr. Hatch resides in London.

"IN THE LAND WHERE COTTON IS KING"
"THINKING OF THEE"
"THE GIRL YOU NEVER HAVE MET"
Harry H. Pace(a) and W. C. Handy(c) (ASCAP).

Mr. Pace was formerly president of the Pace and Handy Music Co., now Handy Brothers Music Co., Inc.; also the Black Swan Record and Pace Phonograph Record Co., Inc. He is now president of the Supreme Liberty Life Insurance Co., of Chicago.

"YOUR TROUBLES WILL BE LIKE MINE"
Salem Tutt Whitney is the author of many songs and books. He will be remembered for his characterization of "Noah" in "The Green Pastures." With his brother, Homer Tutt, he produced many successful shows but is better known by the musical comedy "The Smart Set Company."

"FAT AND GREASY"
Porter Grainger is the writer of "Cotton," "Tain't Nobody's Business If I Do," etc.

Charlie Johnson(c) is one of our most successful orchestra leaders.

"DEEP DAWN"
Claude Hopkins(c) and J. C. Johnson(ASCAP).

Claude Hopkins needs no introduction to radio fans.

"MY DREAMS"
Don Redman and Mercer Cook(c).

Don Redman has written and arranged many songs which you have heard over the air played by his famous band.

Mercer Cook, son of Will Marion Cook and Abbey Mitchell, is the writer of "Stop The Sun, Stop The Moon" (My Gal's Gone), etc.

"A RHYTHM EXCURSION"
Alexander Hill*(ASCAP). See "A Song" (How The First Song Was Born).

"ST. VITUS DANCE"
Maceo Jefferson(c), musician and arranger; well known in Europe and America.

12

COMPOSERS OF POPULAR MUSIC (Continued)

"YOUNG BLACK JOE"
"LET ME TAKE MY GAL WITH ME"

Charles Warfield and Joe Sims.

"SYMPATHIZING MOON"
Henry (Teenan) Jones and Fred Irvin.

"EVERYTIME I PICK A SWEETIE"
Allie Moore*(c) was formerly a Broadway publisher.

BLUES COMPOSERS

"LONESOME ROAD BLUES"
"SNAKEY BLUES"

Will Nash was among the pioneers as "Blues" composer-pianist.

"PEE GEE BLUES"
H. Quali Clark*(c) and Alex Rogers*(c).
This composition is dedicated to P. G. Lowery, cornet soloist.
H. Quali Clark was the author of "Shake It And Break It," "Insect Ball," "You Can't Keep A Good Girl Down," "You'll Think Of Me."

"FLORIDA BLUES"
William King Phillips*(c) was formerly clarinetist and saxophonist with Handy's original band of Memphis.

BLUES COMPOSERS (Continued)

"STINGAREE BLUES"

Clinton Kemp.

"WEST TEXAS BLUES"
Charles Booker, writer of "Osceola Blues," "Pencil Papa Blues," "A Woman Gets Tired Of One Man All The Time"—originally published by Yancey & Booker, Memphis, Tenn.

"BLIND MAN BLUES"
Eddie Green(c) and Billie McLaurie(c).
Eddie Green(c) is better known by "A Good Man Is Hard To Find."
Billie McLaurie was a showman in the days of "String Beans"—pioneer "blues" singer.

"MEMPHIS BLUES"
"ST. LOUIS BLUES"
"BEALE STREET BLUES"
"YELLOW DOG BLUES"
"JOE TURNER BLUES"
"OLE MISS"
"HARLEM BLUES"
"AUNT HAGAR'S CHILDREN"
"HESITATING BLUES"

W. C. Handy is the originator of the "Blues." He is the founder of Pace and Handy Music Co., Inc., now Handy Brothers Music Co., Inc., as successors.

COMPOSERS OF MOTION PICTURE MUSIC

"LOOKIN' FOR MY LONG LOST GAL OR MAN"

Harvey Brooks(c) is the writer of much of the music for Mae West's productions.

————

"I GO CONGO"
"LAZY RAIN"

Clarence Muse is known throughout America as a producer of shows and revues but better known as a screen star in Warner Brothers' Productions, his first appearance being in "Hearts In Dixie." He is the writer of "Sleepy Time Down South."

FEMALE COMPOSERS

"DEEP RIVER BLUES"
Lucile Handy Springer(c) is the daughter of W. C. Handy.

————

"THE KITCHENETTE ACROSS THE HALL"

Ruth Moore (c), of Milwaukee, has written a number of cute songs played and sung on phonograph records.

————

"THINK OF ME LITTLE DADDY"

Bert (Alberta) Whitman(c) is one of the "Whitman Sisters," known for their splendid shows throughout the country. She is the daughter of a Methodist minister and the writer of many songs.

————

"STAY"

Elizabeth Handy White (c) is one of the daughters of W. C. Handy.

14

"OLE MAN SWANEE"

Irene Higginbotham (c), (nom de plume—Hart Jones).

"FRIENDLESS BLUES"

Mercedes Gilbert(a), one of the prominent characters in "The Green Pastures" and leading character in "Mulatto."

COMPOSERS OF COMIC SONGS

"WHO BROKE THE LOCK ON THE HEN HOUSE DOOR"

Henry Troy(a) and Irving (Sneeze) Williams(c).

Irving (Sneeze) Williams, formerly president of the Clef Club.

Henry Troy is known to all America for introducing "Just One Word Of Consolation" and the vaudeville act of Smith and Troy.

"THE UNBELIEVER"

Chris Smith, Fred'k M. Bryan and Bert Williams.

THE RODMAN WANAMAKER MUSIC COMPOSITION CONTEST

Offered by "The Robert Curtis Ogden Association," The Wanamaker Store, Philadelphia, Pa., and sponsored by The National Association of Negro Musicians, Inc.

LIST OF ANNUAL WINNERS
First Contest — 1927

CLASS I	Let Freedom's Music Ring	Wellington Adams
CLASS II	A Love Song	Frank Tizol
	A Love Song	Harry R. Rush
CLASS III	Spiritual Lullaby	Fred M. Bryan
	Evenin'	Hinton Jones
	Twilight Melody	Wesley Howard
	Mammy Lov's Her Li'l' Black Child	Wellington Adams
CLASS IV	Prestidigitation (title omitted)	Maude O. Bonner
	Prestidigitation	J. Harold Brown
	Prestidigitation	Richard Oliver
	The Hail Storm	Fred D. Griffin
	The Brook	Mrs. C. B. Cooley
CLASS V	(title omitted)	Oscar Howard
	Theme and Variations	John A. Gray
	Loyalty's Gift	George Duckett

Second Contest — 1928

CLASS I	Rondo Intermezzo	Francisco Tizol
	Wade in the Water	J. Harold Brown
	Oh Ye Ethiopia	Fred D. Griffith
CLASS II	I Think Of Thee	Blanche K. Thomas
	Just When I Thought	Edward Gongalia
	Carry Me Back to de Southlan'	Max Davis
CLASS III	Rhapsody	J. Harold Brown
	Etude Etienne	John A. Gray
	The Runaway Slave	George Duckett
CLASS IV	March Triumph of the West	Fred Griffin
	E Flat Major	Charles Hammock
	The Fidelity March	Cornelius W. Gaylord

Third Contest — 1930

CLASS I	Jump Back Honey	William L. Dawson
	Hinder Me Not	Penman Lovingood

16

CLASS II	Scherzo	William L. Dawson
	Negro Folk Suite	Major N. Clark Smith
CLASS III	Wade In The Water	Druscilla T. Altwell
	Negro Folk Song Prelude	Major N. Clark Smith
CLASS IV	African Chief	J. Harold Brown

Fourth Contest — 1931

CLASS I	Lovers Plighted	William L. Dawson
	Sandals	James E. Dorsey
Honorable Mention, Break, Break Hill		Friends of the People, Hampton, Va.
	There's Victory I Must Gain	Rek Narf, Kansas, Mo.
CLASS II	Allegro	J. Harold Brown
	Sonata	Eugene A. Burkes
Honorable Mention—Cotton Dance		Florence B. Price
	A Dance In Brown	Margaret A. Bonds
CLASS III	String Quartet In A Minor	J. Harold Brown
	Sweet Low, Sweet Chariot	N. Clark Smith
Honorable Mention—I Am Troubled in Mind		Blanche K. Thomas
	Feed My Sleep	Wellington Adams
CLASS IV	Carried over until 1932.	

Fifth Contest — 1932

CLASS IV	A Symphonic work—carried over from 1931	
	First Prize—Symphony in E Minor	Florence B. Price
Honorable Mention—Autumn Moods		J. Harold Brown
	Ethiopia's Shadow in America	Florence B. Price
CLASS II	Piano Composition	
	Sonata in E Minor	Florence B. Price
Honorable Mention—Fantasie No. 4		Florence B. Price
	Moon Revel	Hugo Bornn
CLASS I	The Sea Ghost	Margaret Allison Bond
Honorable Mention—Lamentation		Eric Franker
	Hymn of the Universe	G. Raymond Smith

SOME OF THE WRITERS WHO HAVE CONTRIBUTED TO

CLARENCE WILLIAMS' CATALOG

(Code** unpublished—on records only)

ARMSTRONG, LOUIS(c)—"Where Did You Stay Last Night," "Coal Cart Blues."

ARMSTRONG, LILLIAN(c)—"After Tonight."

BROOKS, SHELTON(c)—"Smile Your Blusies Away," "Hole In The Wall."

BOOKER, ARTHUR(c)—"I've Got The Sweetest Little Sweetie."**
BOOKER, CHARLES(c)—"Osceola Blues," "Pencil Papa."**
BECHET, SIDNEY(c)—"Ghost Of the Blues."
BRYMN, TIM(c)—"Shout Sister Shout."

BLAKE, EUBIE & PORTER, ARTHUR(c)—"Blues, Why Don't You Let Me Alone."

BISHOP, WALTER(c)—"Swing Brother Swing," "Dispossessin' Me."
BRADFORD, PERRY(c)—"Crazy Blues."

BIGEOU, ESTHER—"T. P. Valley Blues," "Panama Limited Blues."**

BAQUET, GEORGE F.—"My Music Man," "Bessie's Got the Blues."**

BENBOW, WILLIAM—"Memphis Bound," "Just Because I'm A Teasin' Brown."**

BOCAGE, PETER—"Mama's Gone Goodbye."
BROWN, J. E.—"Castaway."
BARGER, MYRTLE—"My Best Man Has Stolen My Man And Gone."**

BROWN & DUMONT—"Send Me A Man," "Let's Do It Again."**

CHRISTIAN, BUDDIE—"Dark Eyes I'm In Love With You," "Sugar House Stomp."

CHAPPELLE & STINNETTE(c)—"I Wish You Would."
COX, JIMMY(c)—"Last Go Round Blues."
DAVENPORT, CHARLES--"Cow Cow Blues,"

DOWELL, EDGAR & MAMIE MEDINA(c)—"Dada Strain," "It Makes No Difference Now."

DORSEY, THOMAS & LLOYD—"Eagle Rock Me Papa."
EASTON, SIDNEY—"Token In De Land."
FOWLER, LEMUEL(c)—"Fowler Twist," "Cruel Backbitin' Blues."
FLETCHER, LUCY(c)—"Sugar Blues," (co-writer).

GRAY, SAM—"Jealous Hearted Blues," "Bed Time Blues."

GEORGE, HORACE—"If I Live and Nothing Happens."

GAINES, CHARLIE—"I Can't Dance Got Ants In My Pants."

GILBERT, MERCEDES(c)—"Decatur Street Blues," "Also Ran Blues."

GRAINGER, PORTER(c)—"Tain't Nobody's Bizness If I Do."

GREEN, EDDIE(c)—"You've Got The Right Key But The Wrong Key Hole."

HOPES, WILLIAM BOOTS—"A Brownskin Is The Best Gal After All."

HIGGINS, BILLY—"Early Every Morning."**

HAYES, CLIFFORD—"Jug Band Blues."**

HAMMED, TASHUA—"Echo Of Spring," "Let Every Day Be Mother's Day."

HENDERSON, FLETCHER(c)—"Tozo."

HEYWOOD, DONALD(c)—"Come On Home."

HILL, ALEX(c)—"Shout Sister Shout."

IRVING, ROLAND C.—"How Can I Love When You Keep On, etc."

JEFFERSON, MACEO(c)—"Whoop It Up And Break It Down."**

JORDAN, JOE(c)—"Morocco Blues," "Anytime."

JOHNSON, FREDDIE(c)—"Absence Makes The Heart Grow Fonder."**

JOHNSON, JAMES P.(c)—"Carolina Shout."

JOHNSON, LUCKIE(c)—"Everything I Tell You, You Go And Tell Your Monkey Man."**

JOHNSON, J. C.(c)—"Never Mind About Me," "From Now On."

JONES, RICHARD M.—"Jazzin' Babies Blues," "I'm Lonesome, Nobody Cares For Me."

JEFFERSON, GEORGE—"Irresistible Blues."

JENKINS, HEZEKIAH—"Mouth Organ Blues," "Hen Pecked Blues."

JACKSON, MIKE—"Candy Lips I'm Stuck On You," "Keyboard Express."

LISTON, VIRGINIA—"Jealous Hearted Blues," "Put Your Mind On No One Man."

LILLARD, JAMES—"You, Just You," "I'm Glad You're Lonesome."

MEDINA, MAMIE—"That Da Da Strain," "Struttin' Along."

MORGAN, W. ASTOR(c)—"Love Is Like A Bubble," "Somebody's Knocking At Your Door."

MACK, CECIL(c)—"Fly 'Round Young Ladies," "You For Me, Me For You."

19

MARTIN, SARAH—"Mama's Got The Blues."
MORRIS, THOMAS—"E Flat Blues," "Original Charleston Strut."
MATSON, CHAS.—"Stop Shimmying Sister," "Windy City Blues."
MANNING, SAM—"Brown Boy."

OVERSTREET, BENTON(c)—"Play It A Long Time Papa."
OLIVER, JOE(c)—"West End Blues."

POTTER, ANNIE S.—"Shreveport Blues."
PAYTON, LEW(c)—"All The Wrongs You've Done To Me."
PINKARD, MACEO(c)—"Pile of Logs and Stone Called Home,"
    "Livin' High."

PEYTON, DAVE—"Lonesome Woman Blues."

RUSSELL, WILL & ED. HERBERT(c)—"Oh Daddy Blues."
RAZAF, ANDY(c)—"Nobody But My Baby Is Getting My Love."
REDMAN, DON (c)—"I Don't Like The Way You Do."
SMITH, BESSIE—"Jail House Blues."
SIMMONS, ROSSEAU—"He's Just As Much Mine As Yours."
STEWART, JAMES—"Window Shoppin' Blues."
SMITH, WILLIE—"The Swamp," "The Stuff Is Here and Mellow."
SIMS, JOE—"The World Is Round It's Crooked."
SMITH, CHRIS(c),—"Cakewalking Babies From Home."
SIMMONS, ROUSSEAU(c)—"Who'll Chop Your Suey When I'm
    Gone."

THOMAS, GEORGE—"New Orleans Hop Scop Blues," "Sweet Baby
    Doll."
THOMPSON, DEKOVEN(c)—"House Rent Stomp."**
TODD, CLARENCE(c)—"Papa De Da Da."
TYUS, CHARLES & EFFIE(c)—"Omaha Blues."
TROY, HENRY(c)—"Cakewalking Babies From Home."
TRENT, JOE(c)—"I'm Going Back To Bottomland."

WARFIELD, CHARLES—"Baby Won't You Please Come Home,"
    "Daddy, How I Miss You Since You've Gone."
WALLACE, SIPPY—"Can Anybody Take Sweet Mama's Place,"
    "Stranger's Blues."
WILSON, DANIEL—"Mama Stayed Out The Whole Night," "How
    Could I Be Blue."
WALLER, THOMAS "FATS"(c)—"Squeeze Me," "Senorita Mine."
WILLIAMS, SPENCER(c)—"Everybody Loves My Baby," "I've
    Found A New Baby."
WOODING, SAM(c)—"Southern Blues," "Changeable Blues."**
WEAVER, SYLVESTER(c)—"Guitar Blues."**

OTHER COMPOSERS OF WORTHWHILE MENTION WHO ARE NOT MEMBERS OF THIS SOCIETY AND WHOSE WORKS WE DO NOT PUBLISH ARE:

ALLEN, BUD(c)—Co-writer "Georgia Grind." Published "Chicago Blues," "Midnight Blues."

BIVANS, NATHAN*(c)—"Deed I Ain't Seen No Messenger Boy," etc.

BLAND, JAMES*(c)—"Carry Me Back To Old Virginny," "Oh Dem Golden Slippers," "Climbing Up The Golden Stairs," "In The Evening By The Moonlight."

BOATNER, EDWARD(c)—One of the first to record spirituals as an artist on George W. Broun records, a race enterprise; a well known composer.

BRADFORD, PERRY(c)—Music Publisher. "Crazy Blues," "You Can't Keep A Good Man Down," "That Thing Called Love," etc.

BRIGGS, WILLIAM H.(c)—"Reflections."

BROWN, AL*(c)—"I'm Going To Break Up This Jamboree."

CALLOWAY, CAB(c)—Better known by "Minnie The Moocha."

CARTER, BENNY(c)—"Blues In My Heart," etc.

CHARLTON, MELVILLE(c)—"Erotique." One of our outstanding organists.

COOKE, CHARLES L.(c)—"Blame It On The Blues," "Daisy Days."

CROSS, ELIJAH(c)—"Missouri Maize."

DABNEY, FORD(c)—"Porto Rican Dance," and "Shine" in collaboration with Cecil McPherson.

DAWSON, WILLIAM L.(c)—Conducted a chorus of 100 voices from Tuskegee and his symphony founded on spirituals was performed at the opening of Radio City. A few of his works are "Forever Thine," "My Lord What A Morning," "Talk About A Child That Do Love Jesus Here Is One," etc.

DITON, CARL(c)—Compositions for Mixed choruses, vocal solos, pipe organ, based on Negro spirituals. A few of his works are: "Swing Low, Sweet Chariot," for the organ, and "Little David Play On Your Harp" for chorus.

DIXON, WILL H.*(c)—"Brazilian Dreams," "Crazy 'Bout You" and other romantic songs.

DUNBAR, PAUL LAWRENCE*(a) — Poet. "Who Dat Said Chicken In This Crowd?" "Exhortation," "Swing Along," musical settings by Will Marion Cook.

EDMUNDS, SHEPARD N.(c)—"I Was There And I Had No Business To Be There," "Deed I Do," "I've Got Something I've Been Saving For You."

EUROPE, JAMES REESE*(c)—"Castle Walk," "Clef Club March," etc.

GREENE, SAM*(c)—"Murmuring Voices Of The Deep," written in 1870.

HANDY, WILL(c) (nom de plume for Cole & Johnson)—"Didn't He Ramble."

HARE, MAUD-CUNEY*(c)—An Authority on Creole Music; author of "Negro Musicians and Their Music."

HARVEY, HEBRON(c)—"Dawn," "Longing," in collaboration with Paul Lawrence Dunbar.

HASKELL, PROF. ANTONIO LEE(c) of St. Louis, Mo.—Negro folk Songs.

HENDERSON, FLETCHER(c)—"Stampede," "Where," etc.

HILL, J. LUBRIE* (Producer)—"My Dahomian Queen," "Manhattan Rag," "At The Ball," "Rock Me In The Cradle Of Love" and many other production numbers.

HOGAN, ERNEST*(c) (Real name Ruben Crowder)—"All Coons Look Alike To Me," "Enjoy Yourselves," "The Congregation Will Please Keep Your Seat," etc. He was the leading comedian of his time.

HUNTER, CHARLES A.(c)—"Ada My Sweet Potato" and some of the music in "Ghost of The Red Moon."

JACKSON, TONY*(c)—Better known by "Pretty Baby."

JESSYE, EVA(c)—A Book of Spirituals.

JOHNS, AL*(c)—Better known by "Honey Lamb."

JONES, CLARENCE M.(c)—"One Wonderful Night," "Amid The Pyramids," "Who Dat Said Who Dat." Pianist with the Southernaires over the National Broadcasting System.

JOHNSON, HAVEN(c)—"My Last Affair."

JOPLIN, SCOTT*(c)—"Maple Leaf Rag," "Sun Flower Drag," Euphonic Sounds" and an opera, "Tremonisha." He was "king of ragtime."

JORDAN, JOE(c)—Better known by "Sweetie Dear."

KELLEY, H. ALF(c), who wrote in collaboration with J. Paul Wyer the song, "A Bunch of Blues," etc.

KIRK, ANDY(a)—Co-author "Till The Real Thing Comes Along."

LEW, W. E.(c)—Pioneer composer. Formerly accompanist to Madame Marie Selika and coach to Madame Flora Batson-Bergen and Sissiretta Jones (Black Patti). Collaborated with Hallback in "Alabama Sue," 1903.

LUCAS, SAM(c)—Affectionately referred to as "Dad Lucas." A book containing eight (8) Minstrel Songs, published by White, Smith & Co., 1884. Dean of the theatrical profession. "Carve That Possum," "Grandfather's Clock," "Shivering, Shaking Out In The Cold."

MATTHEWS, ARTIE(c), "Weary Blues" and Spirituals.

NICKERSON, CAMILLE(c)—An authority on Creole Music. President of the National Association of Negro Musicians, Inc., 1936-37.

OLIVER, JOE(c), "Dr. Jazz," "Sugar Foot Stomp," etc.

OWSLEY, TIM (c)—"I Got Good Common Sense" and others. He was a successful showman.

PIRON, ARMAND, J.(c)—"Shimmy Like Sister Kate," "Brownskin," "I Can Beat You Doing What You're Doing Me." Mr. Piron was formerly partner in Williams and Piron Publishing Co., of New Orleans.

ROBERTS, LUCKY(c)—"Junk Man Rag," etc.

SAMPSON, EDGAR(c)—"Stompin' At The Savoy."

SEALS, BABY(c)—Pioneer "Blues" composer. "Baby Seals Blues."

SELMOUR, C.(c)—"Panama Rag."

SHIPP, JESSYE A.*(c)—Produced much of the material for the "Williams and Walker" shows and had a prominent part in "The Green Pastures." "The Man In The Moon Might Tell."

SMART and WILLIAMS(c)—Vaudeville team before the days of "Williams and Walker." "That Ain't No Talk To Give Me."

SMITH N. CLARK*(c)—"Black Patti Waltz" and several symphonies based on pure African melodies obtained while touring the dark continent. An arranger of many traditional spirituals.

SPIKES BROS. and CARTER(c)—"Some Day Sweetheart," etc.

STILL, WILLIAM GRANT(c)—"Africa," a symphonic poem; "Afro-American symphony"; the opera "Blue Steel" and twelve Negro spirituals in two volumes (the latter published by Handy Bros. Music Co.,), etc.

STONE, FRED(c)—"My Ragtime Baby."

THOMPSON, DEKOVEN(c)—"If I Forget," "This Time To-morrow."

TURPIN, CHARLES and TOM*(c)—St. Louis composers who wrote many dance tunes such as "Easy Winners," "St. Louis Rag."

TYLER, GERALD(c)—"Ships That Pass In The Night."

WHITE, CLARENCE CAMERON(c)—"March Triumphal." A book of forty spirituals entitled "Bandanna sketches."

WILLIAMS, BERT*(c) was our greatest comedian of all times. "Nobody," "Unbeliever," etc.

WORK, FREDERICK J. and JOHN W.(c)—Pioneers on books of Negro Folk Songs.

WILLIAMS & WALKER(c)—"The Ghost Of A Coon," "Why Don't You Get A Lady Of Your Own."

BIBLIOGRAPHY

Note:

In compiling this work some names may have been overlooked and yet, it is the most exhaustive published. We trust the reader will appreciate this limited service and thank you for any such omissions you may point out that future lists might be complete.

For more light on the works of outstanding composers we respectfully refer you to the following books:

WHO'S WHO IN COLORED AMERICA...............Thomas Yenser

THEY AI L SANG ....E. B. Marks

JAZZ ....Paul Whiteman

BLUES—An Anthology
    Edited by ....W. C. Handy
    With Introduction by ....E. Abbe Niles
    Published by ....A. & C. Boni, Inc.

NEGRO YEAR BOOK ....Monroe N. Work

BOOK OF AMERICAN NEGRO POETRY ......James Weldon Johnson

TIN PAN ALLEY ....Isaac Goldberg

THE NEW NEGRO ....Alain Locke

THE NEGRO IN OUR HISTORY ....Carter Godwin Woodson

THE NEGRO AND HIS MUSIC ....Alain Locke

NEGRO MUSICIANS AND THEIR MUSIC...............Maud Cuney-Hare